Surf Fishing

The Light-Line Revolution

The Complete Guide To
Surf Fishing The California Coast

Surf Fishing

The Light-Line Revolution

Bill Varney, Jr.

www.fishthesurf.com
Long Beach, CA

The information contained in this book was compiled over
a lifetime and is meant to be used as a guide to local
California surf fishing.

This book contains information gathered from several sources and has
been reviewed and edited. The publisher, author and editors do not
guarantee the book's accuracy and assume no responsibility for injury or
property damage resulting from the use of this book's contents.

Because fishing, as with most sports, is inherently dangerous, become
familiar with your equipment, watch the weather and be respectful
and cognizant of your surroundings.

Copyright ©2006 by Bill Varney Jr.
All rights reserved
No part of this book may be used or reproduced in any manner
whatsoever without the written permission of the publisher,
except for the inclusion of a brief quotation in a review.

Published and printed in the United States of America

Cover Photo pictures and Illustrations by Bill Varney Jr.

Field Research Partners: Ken Vanwuyckhuyse,
Kevin Vliet, Ed Smith and Brad Baier.

Books available at:
www.fishthesurf.com
Bill Varney Jr.
4501 E. Pacific Coast Hwy. #600
Long Beach, CA 90804
(714) 377-9001

IBSN 0-9772486-0-7
(978-09772486-0-5)

First Edition

Cover and interior design by www.KarenRoss.com

To my wife Kristen,

For her immeasurable patience

To my father

For his introduction to the ocean

To my mother for her support of my dreams

And to my kids and all children

For their contagious enthusiasm to

Learn everything the sea

Has to offer.

Table of Contents

Quotes 9
Introduction 11

1. **Fish Of The Surf** 15
    Types of surf fish
    Strikes
    Best baits
    Best spots
    Rig up

2. **Fishing Beaches And Rocky Shores** 33
    Gear for sandy beaches
    Fishing sandy beaches
    Gear for rocky shores
    Fishing rocky shores

3. **Bait** 51
    Types of bait
    Catching bait
    Keeping bait alive
    Hooking various baits
    Freezing and storing bait

4. **Gear Up** 85
    Lines and leaders
    Sinkers
    Swivels
    Hooks
    Beads
    Knot tying
    Rigging

5. **Taking Control** 101
   Fighting the fish
   Fishing in the wind

6. **Tide And Moon** 105
   What causes tides
   What tide is best for surf fishing
   How to read tide charts
   Tides and the time of day
   The moon's affect on surf fishing

7. **Catch And Release** 113
   How to safely release fish

Surf Fish Calendar 115
Appendix

Herbert Hoover
"Fishing is a discipline in the equality of men, for all men are equal before fish."

John Buchan
"The charm of fishing is that it is the pursuit of something that is elusive but attainable, a perpetual series of occasions for hope."

Thomas D'urfey
"Of all the world's enjoyments that
ever valued were,
There's none of our employments
with fishing can compare."

Introduction

In the beginning:
Oh boy, it's sure a long way down! The sun is beginning to set and it's every color in the world. As dad reels the line up it comes over the edge with one, two, three bare hooks and suddenly a jumpy little fish. I'm three, and my dad is patiently trying to teach me how to fish from the Redondo horseshoe pier.

Most other days, we'd stop by Jerry's Tackle Box or Red's get bait, our long rods and go fishing at the beach. Dad would put a three-ounce pyramid sinker on the line and cast it out as far as the eye could see. Occasionally, we caught a good fish, but most of the time it was kelp and fought like a sinking car.

Later on:
In the dark, shortly before the sun began to rise, I would ride my bike to the pier to fish for perch. The butt of my rod was fastened inside and "Alpo" dog food can bolted to the right side of my front tire. On my back was a knapsack crammed full of tackle and food.

Once there, we'd climb under the pier and fish up against the pilings for perch. One day, when we ran out of bait. I pulled a sidewinder crab from the piling, pinned it on the hook, and let my line out. Upon hitting the water, a shadow swam out from under the dock, clamped onto the crab, and almost pulled me into the water.

Today:
I'm scrambling up the rocks because a big wave is coming and I know I'll get wet. But it's okay, my gear is light and I'm out of the wave's path in time.

It's a workday and almost everyone's at the job. I have the whole beach to myself. Today I'm fishing with the lightest gear possible. My rod is eight feet long and weighs only twenty-ounces. I use four pound pink line on a reel that almost fits in my front pocket. All the gear and bait I'll ever need is in a small hook wallet hanging around my neck.

Sorry, it's time to go now.
Yeah ! I think I'm getting a bite.

Take everything you learn from this book and expand upon it. Do feel free to try your own fishing experiments and refine your light- line technique. The knowledge you'll learn from this book was compiled from years of local surf fishing and a lot of good people who were brave enough to share what they know with all of us.

As a teenager my education continued thanks to the help of notable fisherman Jerry Morris, Fred Oakley, Hap Jacobs, John Dipley, Pineapple, Wesley Strong, Red and the owners of *TC Bait and Tackle* where I worked.

Tight lines and good fishing,

Bill

CHAPTER 1

Fish of the Surf

In This Chapter:

**Types of surf fish
Strikes
Best baits
Best spots
Rig up**

Our first chapter serves as an introduction to the fish that live in the California surf.

California Corbina (menticirrhus undulatus)

Pound for pound corbina are the best fighting fish in the California surf.

A strong and aggressive fish, the corbina strikes bait on the run. Their favorite meals include mussels, calms and bloodworms—but their main diet consists of sand crabs. Corbina feed in shallow water by running their barbell across the bottom to search for sand crabs and clams. The fish frequently float in just inches of water and folks are often surprised when one swims between their legs. They use the incoming tide and wave motion to search for soft crabs. In just inches of water, they float suspended in the inshore trough waiting for their chance to charge the beach.

Corbina live from Santa Barbara to Cabo San Lucas. On a recent trip to Mexico's East Cape I learned first-hand that Baja has some of the best croaker fishing in the world. Go diving in the East Cape and you'll see hundreds of schooling croaker swim beneath you creating a huge carpet across the ocean floor.

Another great place to get a look at these fish is from your local pier during an incoming tide. It's not uncommon to see four or five at times, just inches away from swimmers!

Although most corbina are found near shore they have been caught in nearly eighty feet of water. Marine biologists believe corbina can grow to about thirty-two inches. A twelve-inch corbina is roughly three years old. A twenty-inch fish weighing roughly four pounds is about nine years old.

During winter (November through April) corbina migrate away from the beach. When spring rolls around in May, they spawn through September and are everywhere in the surf.

The largest corbina feed on the largest soft sand crabs. These crabs are most numerous during the warm water months of July, August and September. Corbina rarely run in large schools and are usually found alone or with no more than two other fish.

STRIKE: Very distinctive—they inhale the bait and immediately swim away. Rather than a nibble, like with perch, the corbina picks up the bait, straightens the line and quickly swims away. There is no question when they are on the other end!

Corbina Tip:
Fish flatter sloping beaches on a rising tide

BEST SPOT: Inshore, twenty feet from the dry sand in the inshore trough. Sometimes corbina may also be found a bit farther out near the wave impact zone where another trough has formed. Flatter, more sloping beaches, are best. Fish are found in as few as 6" of water.

BEST BAIT: Soft shell sand crab and bloodworms

RIG UP: (Carolina Rig, see chap. 4) Sliding quarter, to as much as, a one ounce egg sinker, bead, swivel, eighteen inch leader of four pound test and a number two to six (depending on the size of bait) snelled octopus (offset) hook.

Yellowfin Croaker (Umbrina Roncador)

Not unlike other croaker (corbina, seabass) yellowfin also have a distinctive goatee barbell. Shiny gray and silver in color they are more rounded and flat like a bar perch. Yet they have very distinctive yellow fins on the top (dorsal) and bottom (anal fin). Larger yellowfin commonly have green, blue, and brown oblique stripes.

Yellowfin can be caught from Ventura to the tip of Baja. They stay in water shallower than twenty-five feet (although they have been caught in more than fifty feet) and congregate in medium to large schools. Although they can be found in inches of water some of our best bites have been in deeper water near the outside trough created beneath the wave impact zone.

The yellowfin is a very aggressive feeder. Its strike is surprisingly strong. Not unlike corbina, yellowfin spawn from May to September. They can be caught all year long along the coast. Some of your best and at times wide open bites, will be just following their spawn in late summer.

The yellowfin grows to about twenty inches. A fish this size would be about ten years old. One half that size is about four years old.

STRIKE: When a yellowfin picks up your bait you know it! One of the strongest strikes for the size of fish—they will usually pick up you bait with a strong nibble and swim away immediately.

BEST SPOTS: Unlike corbina, yellowfin croaker are schooling fish and are sometimes found in large schools of one thousand or more. They are found close to shore in the surf line, and outside the surf line in up to sixty feet of water.

In late summer fish school in large numbers to chase small bait and feed. These schools consist of like sized fish that are veracious eaters. It's not uncommon to catch as many as one per minute when they go into a crazed post-spawn hunt!

BEST BAIT: Both live and artificial baits work well for yellowfin croaker. Sand crabs, ghost shrimp, bloodworms and mussel work well. Artificial lures such as small spoons, spinners and grubs will also do the job.

RIG UP: Most fish weigh in the one pound to three-pound range. The sliding rig, using a small egg sinker, works best for bait and grub applications. For lures like spoons and flashers, use a direct mono knot. The ganion grub rig is also productive when the bite is very hot.

Barred Surfperch (Amphistichus Argenteus)

The first word in the name "surf" perch tells us a lot about this little fish. With two rows of teeth it is well known as a forager. Its teeth allow it to catch and crush a variety of baits. In fact, not unlike the barred sand bass, perch can also pick up small clams and encased worms and conveniently crush their shells to reach their soft interior. All the while surfing the waves back and forth in the shallow inshore surf.

The barred surfperch is characterized by a set of brassy diagonal bars outlined in light green stripes. Occasionally, in the colder water years, you may catch the Red Tail Surfperch with its distinctive red fins perched upon the unmistakable surfperch shape.

Because barred surfperch enjoy a variety of water temperatures they can be found from Canada to the tip of Baja. Perch migrate from shallow water to deep water in mid summer looking for a cool spot to rest. In winter and spring they move into the shallows to feed and spawn.

Perch can be caught in as little as two inches of water. Like yellowfin croaker, perch also roam in schools but do not generally range far distances. Barred surfperch grow to roughly seventeen inches or about four pounds. Females grow quicker than males with a twelve-inch fish being about five years old.

BEST SPOT: Barred surfperch live in the inshore trough moving in and out with the surge of surf. The churning action dredges up clams, crabs and pieces of food. They are very close to shore usually within sixty feet or less. Many fish are caught in less than four inches of water!

BEST BAIT: Both natural and artificial lures work well. Perch eat sand crabs, mussel, ghost shrimp, bloodworm, plastic grubs, and flies such as the *Clauser Minnow*.

During wintertime, when food is scarce, perch are very aggressive toward the small plastic grub. Later, in spring and summer, perch are scarcer and prefer natural bait. Not unlike most inshore surf fish they love soft-shell sand crabs.

STRIKE: As mentioned earlier, the surfperch, with its two sets of teeth, is a food grinder. The bite is normally a series of nibbles followed by a strong pull. Because perch inhale and exhale their bait it is best to set the hook following the first set of nibbles.

RIG UP: Once again the Carolina Rig (sliding rig) works well for both bait and grubs. In small surf, go without a sliding weight and try a tiny pinch-on weight (like a split shot or Gremlin®). Fish for perch on two to six pound, green or pink monofilament.

Walleye Surfperch (Hyperprosopon Argenteum)

Walleye surfperch are easily distinguished from other Southern California surfperch. Silver in color, they have larger than normal eyes, blue accents at the top of their back and black tipped tail fins.

Their upturned mouth may be the reason for their feisty nibble. Scientists have found these fish in as deep as six hundred feet of water, although most are caught in the shallow waters of the inshore trough.

Because they congregate in schools they may be concentrated in one area. Although you will rarely find one larger then eight to ten inches, once in a while you'll catch one that's a hefty twelve inches and about six years old. Walleye, like barred surfperch, can be found on sandy beaches and rocky shores near jetties, piers and landings.

BEST SPOT: Walleye congregate in schools. One of the best spots is in the shallows of the inshore trough where fish wait for worms, clams and sand crabs to be churned in the current. Another good area is near rocks and pier piling structure. Perch live in areas with clean moving water—especially around shore surf, pier pilings and rock outcroppings.

BEST BAIT: As with all fish, perch prefer the bait that occurs naturally throughout their territory. Perch found on sandy beaches will prefer bloodworms and sand crabs from April through September. Perch found around rocks and pilings will prefer mussel and sidewinder crab. *Always look for the bait that best matches what the fish are currently eating.*

When bait is scarce in winter and the water turns colder, perch love the plastic grub. Rig the grub using the same sliding rig. Remember when the surf is bigger, or there is a strong side current, use a heavier sinker and a shorter leader. When the conditions are calm use a lighter sinker and a longer leader. In both cases keep in mind that if you want to get bit, your grub must keep in constant contact with the bottom.

STRIKE: Walleye, like all perch, are nibblers. They move quickly onto bait as it is churned in the tidal zone. But unlike corbina or croaker they do not immediately swim away with the bait. They prefer to inhale and exhale the bait using their large rows of teeth to crush food before swallowing. The exception to this may be in winter when food is scarce and they tend to chew less and swallow more.

Most often the larger the fish the more fierce the strike. Many times, especially in spring, when they are spawning, schools of small fish will nibble and pick your hook clean. But don't be surprised if a much bigger fish hears the commotion and bites. Most walleye surf perch range from one to three pounds.

RIG UP: Again, the Carolina rig will work best in the surf. Your leader should be shorter in strong surf or side current (12 inches) and longer (18-24 inches) in calm waters. Both will insure that your bait stays in contact with the bottom. Use a light one-half ounce sliding sinker in calm conditions and up to an ounce sinker in surging surf.

Leader and main line in either green or pink monofilament in two to six pound test. Walleye also like to strike the small silver Kastmaster® and other small spoon jigs.

California Halibut (Paralichthys Californicus)

The California halibut's most distinguishing characteristic is a pair of eyes on the dark side of the fish. One side of the fish is brown and lightly spotted. The other side, blind by nature, is white. Unlike other flatfish (flounders, sand dabs, etc.) halibut have a row of *very sharp* teeth. Most California halibut are caught between Morro Bay, to the north, and Cabo San Lucas to the south.

Primarily burying themselves in the sand except for their eyes, they love to lay-in-wait for their prey. Most halibut dwell in five feet to two hundred feet of water. Halibut, like other fish, come into the shallows to feed and spawn. With some exceptions, halibut migrate near shore during spring and summer.

In the dead of winter, when prey is scarce and fish are less active, they are usually found in deeper water.

California halibut grow to more than five feet in length. A keeper at twenty-two inches is about five years old. The current California all tackle record (as of the date of publication) is 58 pounds 9 ounces caught at Santa Rosa Island. They have a life span of about 30 years. The older and larger fish (between thirty and fifty pounds) are breeding stock and can rear more young in one year than a fifteen-pound fish can in three years. As such, they are a very valuable resource and should always be released. By far the best eating halibut are those between twenty-two and thirty inches in length (six through twelve pounds).

BEST SPOT: Halibut live where sand meets structure. They will roam in all sandy areas but find the largest share of their food near structure. With the exception of spawn times, these fish usually congregate where they find food. Near a rocky structure area they can be found on the leading edge where the sand meets the rock.

During grunion runs, halibut can be found just off the beach in very shallow water as they track the bait into their spawn area. In the summer months, especially when water is warm, they congregate in shallow water as they chase baitfish like anchovy, smelt, sardine and grunion.

In early spring halibut move in close to shore to spawn. This is the best time to catch these fish at the entrance to local estuaries like the Goleta, Santa Clara and Santa Ana rivermouths, Los Alamitos Bay, Mission Bay and well inside the Long Beach Federal Breakwater. In the dead of winter halibut move to deeper water and are less active along the beach.

Santa Ana Rivermouth

BEST BAIT: Althought halibut have been taken on bloodworms, their favorite foods would include smelt, anchovy and sardine. Live and fresh dead work well.

After casting, retrieve your bait slowly, always keeping in contact with the bottom.

Recently, I witnessed a twelve-pound halibut taken with the *Clauser Minnow fly*. These realistic bait imitations along with two to four inch grubs and swim tail plastics also work well. Not long ago I landed a twenty-two inch halibut on a one and one-half inch motor oil grub — a real departure from the norm. The best colors for grubs and swim baits have been motor oil, olive green with silver fleck, cinnamon with red fleck and other dark colors. Silver spoons such as the Kastmaster and Crocodile also work well.

STRIKE: Halibut rarely hit bait and run. Covered with sand and stuck like glue to the ocean floor they usually bite and hold onto their prey. Slowly they ingest the bait using their very sharp rows of teeth to rake it to pieces. Halibut, unlike other fish such as tuna and yellowtail, prefer their food dead and will usually crush it before ingesting.

Halibut may be one of the hardest fish to hook. One reason is the placement of their mouth. Unlike other fish, they open their mouth on its side and the hook slips out missing the roof or floor. Many anglers use a "trap" rig, which utilizes a small treble hook, or "stinger" hook tied three inches below their main bait hook. If you do use a trap rig be sure to use a non nickel-plated hook so that it can rust out quickly if it needs to be left in the fish.

RIG UP: Whether you're using a grub or live bait, a sliding Carolina Rig works best. Remember to keep the leader short on days with strong waves and currents and longer on calm days. Leaders from twelve to thirty-six inches are best. Tackle up with heavier leader material to reduce the chance of being bit off. Eight to twelve pound leader is ideal. Rod size can also be increased with as much as a twelve-pound main monofilament line when fishing around rocky areas.

When using a "trap" rig tie the "stinger" treble hook three inches from the main bait hook. This can be accomplished by tying a short leader to the eye of the main hook or by leaving an extra long tag line after snelling a hook (I like this best, even when fishing in the boat, because there is one less knot to tie and worry about).

Make sure the "stinger" treble is small and bury at least one of its hook arms into the tail of the bait. This will not only hide the hook but will also help the bait to remain straight and give a more lifelike presentation.

Cast this bait and retrieve it slowly across the bottom. Be aware that the bait needs to be kept in contact with the bottom at all times—so in this case, it's better to use more weight then less.

Other Fish In The Surf

Smelt (Hypomesus Pretiosus)

Sargo (Anis Otremus Davidson)

Stripped Bass (Morone Saxatilis)

Pleagic Stingray (Dasyatis Violacea)

Thornback "Banjo" Shark (Platyrhinoldis Triseriata)

Shovelnose Guitarfish (Rhinobatos Productus)

Leopard Shark (Triakis Semifasciata)

Spotfin Croaker (Roncador Stearnsi)

California Grunion (Leuresthes Tenuis)

And many more…

CHAPTER 2

Fishing Beaches and Rocky Shores

In This Chapter:

**Gear for sandy beaches
Fishing sandy beaches
Gear for rocky shores
Fishing rocky shores**

My favorite two rod and reel combinations include one for sandy beaches with limited rocks and another for rocky areas such as jetties and breakwalls.

GEAR FOR SANDY BEACHES

On sandy beaches there is less chance of entanglement with structure so you can fish much lighter gear and line. Use a 6 to 8-foot spinning rod (i.e. trout rod) with a limber tip. This is the best surf rod for casting, feeling the strike and fighting the fish. Limber rods help the angler with retrieval by keeping the line taught as the fish is brought in through the incoming surf. Look for a rod with a stiff reel seat and a limber tip.

Your spinning reel should have a minimum line capacity of 140 yards of four pound monofilament (a good example would be Shimano® 1000 and 2000 reel series). Because you're on the move, looking for fish, use a hook keeper near the reel seat to hold the hook safe and securely.

Hook Keeper

I spool up with four or six pound test mono. My favorite colors are pink, green and clear. Pink is not everyone's first choice, but its color closely resembles sediment-jumbled water. Because of its stretch and strength pink four-pound test Ande® is my line of choice. I also tie the leaders in four or six pound test. Fluorocarbon line has also been shown to work well as a leader especially in clear water conditions.

FISHING THE BEACH

Never are the rules of observation so important than in fishing. The best and most productive fisherman pay special attention to water, tide and weather conditions.

Once on the beach, surf fisherman must observe beach conditions and determine where the best spot to fish is. Unlike boat fishing it's not as easy as finding a rock to anchor over and catch fish. More subtle observations are made at the beach and once you learn to recognize them you can be assured you will know where the fish are.

When you get to the beach you want to find an area where you can get a good view of the water line. Standing on the beach's berm above the waves is a good place to start. Look up and down the beach. First, look at the beach it self and see how it curves into the water at the shoreline. If you look carefully you will see areas that are points and areas which are bays. The surf, current and tidal movement create these small points or bays.

Subtle differences like these help point out where the fish are living and feeding. Inshore troughs and rip tides work with beach points and bays to make for some of the best fishing spots.

***Tip:** Fan casting, casting your bait in an arch, will allow you to cover more bottom area and take advantage of holes and dips created by tides, currents and waves.*

The Inshore Trough

If you're looking straight out to sea—the inshore trough is twenty to sixty feet in front of you running parallel to the beach. It's usually about six to ten feet wide and two feet deep. In larger surf areas the trough is more pronounced.

The trough is made by the pounding shore break and is the perfect place for fish to hide and search for bait. Corbina lay in wait in the trough and rush up the beach to eat sand crabs. Perch float suspended in the trough and feed on churned up bait.

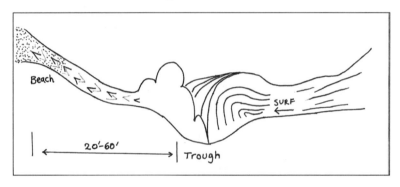

One of the best times to see the inshore trough on your favorite beach is at low tide.

Rip Tide Conditions

Rip tides form when churning waters meet and create an offshore current. It appears with off colored swirling water, rippled areas and possibly foam. Some may be vigorous and obvious while others are subtle. Rip currents normally extend twice or three times as far out as the surf break itself. As they channel water out and away from land they also create a trough perpendicular to the shore. Fish wait in this offshore trough for bait churned up by the rough waters.

A rip tide will pull objects away from the beach and out to sea. On each side of the rip is a neutral pocket formed by an eddy circulation. This eddy makes the rip current the shape of a mushroom.

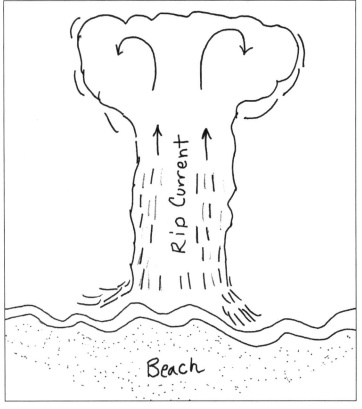

Fish the outside edge of the rip current

The best place to fish a rip current is on its sides casting out and retrieving your bait back along it. Fish will also hide in the area near the top of the mushroom.

Points And Bays

The beach is made up of various points and bays. Some may be hundreds of yards wide or as small as just a few yards apart. Water circulates around these areas and creates fishing opportunities.

Take the vantagepoint above the shore break and look down the beach in each direction. Where on the beach Does the sand extend up and out toward the surf? This is the point.

Point in foreground bay in background

Look and see were the beach comes in and the water floods up the beach in a low area. This is the bay.

The best place to fish on a point is along its sides where the water slows down as the bottom drops off. Waves break along a point in a triangle. The best place to fish is along the edge of the triangle shape. This is where the current created by the breaking waves slows down and releases the bait and particles it carries.

Foam triangle

Points are good areas for walleye and barred surfperch. When fishing the bay, remember that the water and current are moving much slower. Your bait will have much less natural action so slow retrieval is a must. Be sure to keep in contact with the bottom at all times with line tight.

Inshore troughs in the bay are productive for corbina and perch. Try retrieving your bait not only across the trough but along it by walking down the beach. This will keep your bait in the strike zone longer.

Winter And Summer Sand Conditions

Southern California beaches make a remarkable transformation each year as the seasons change and the long-shore current and swells reshape our coastline.

In the summer, swells from the south and southwest push sand northward and onto the beaches. Most areas will gain about forty feet of new sand each summer. This number will be exaggerated in years where strong south swells, generated by hurricanes in Mexico and winter storms in the South Pacific, push even more sand onto our beaches.

This softer sand becomes the home of the sand crab and worm. It reshapes the coastline and accentuates the points and bays described above. Softer sand also allows for a deeper and wider inshore trough.

The summer sands bring their own style of fishing. Crabs are more available and the fish that eat them, such as the corbina, swim in the shallowest water to find them. Look for some of your best fishing in the inshore trough during the summer season.

Winter beach erosion

During the winter, sand recedes from the beach uncovering hidden structure that provides food and becomes home to perch and yellowfin croaker. From December through May, go to your favorite beaches at low tide and find the areas where sand has eroded to expose rock and plant habitat. Throughout winter, fish these spots at a rising high tide and you'll find them to be your most productive fishing areas.

FISHING GEAR FOR ROCKY SHORES

When surf fishing in areas with jetties and breakwall rocks, you'll encounter new challenges which require a change in equipment. Because the chance of entanglement with structure is inevitable your gear must match your surroundings. I use an eight and one-half foot-spinning rod. Once again the tip must be limber to feel the strike, set the hook and get untangled from rocks. Your reel should have a minimum line capacity of two hundred forty yards of twelve pound monofilament line (a 3000 or 4000 series is a good reel size).

I spool up with twelve-pound test line; my favorite colors are clear and green. I use ten or twelve pound leaders. Fluorocarbon leaders come in handy for clear water applications.

A longer and stiffer rod will allow you to cast more weight and be able to pull fish from the rocks. You have a much better chance of hooking a much larger fish from the rocks. Go one time unprepared and you may loose the fish of a lifetime!

Fishing From The Rocks

Rocks and rock jetties come in all shapes and sizes. A series of rocks creates a similar eddy circulation found in rip tides. The outcropping of rock creates an eddy circulation around its point. This is where currents create a natural feeding habitat due to the water movement caused by waves and tidal changes.

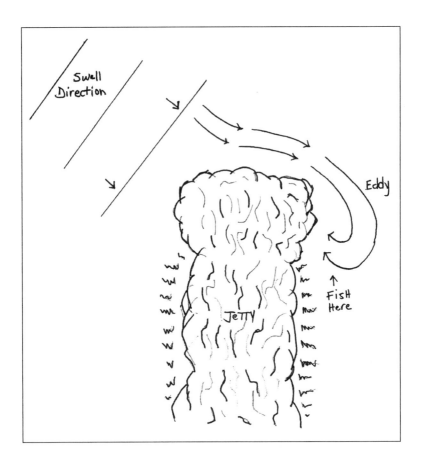

As the tide moves up and down throughout the day water currents vary in strength and intensity. At slack tides, very little water will be moving around rock points. At larger tidal movements, more water and thus larger eddy circulation will occur around rocks.

Eddy circulation is important because it provides a current where fish can suspend themselves while water flushes through their gills providing oxygen.

The eddy also provides a current for bait and nutrients to pass within the fishes' strike zone.

Slack tide conditions create very little circulation and require fish to move from area to area to provide oxygen and search for food. Fishing is always best when there is a slow to moderate current condition. Conditions of no current or a very strong one are least productive and make fishing tough.

Once upon the rock or rock area you'll be fishing, look out toward the point and find the leeward or downside of the current. Look for where the water is going. Look for similar characteristics to the rip current: swirling water rippled areas and possible foam.

Fish the outside and inside edges of the eddy. The outside edge may be toward open water and the inside up against the rocks. This is where the fish will hide, breathing comfortably and waiting for their next meal.

Fish don't like to hide in the fastest moving portion of an eddy. They prefer to stay on the sidelines and wait for your bait!

Unlike most *beach* surf fishing, fishing from the rocks is productive at both high and low tides.

Notes:

CHAPTER 3

Bait

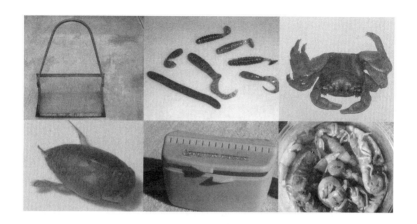

In This Chapter:

**Types of bait
Catching bait
Keeping bait alive
Hooking various baits
Freezing bait**

Everything has a rule or two. Here's rule number one when it comes to which bait to use: Look for what occurs naturally around the area you are fishing.

What's between the rocks or in the sand beneath your feet? Look around and see what you think the fish are eating. If you see mussels on the rocks or crabs in the sand you can be pretty sure that what they're eating.

Sand Crabs (Emerita analoga)

When it comes to surf fishing, if I had only one kind of bait, this would be it. Every surf fish, big or small, searches for one of the billions of soft-shell sand crabs. In spring, when the ocean warms to above 60 degrees, the sand crab emerges and sheds his first shell. Much like a snake sheds its skin as it grows so does the sand crab. Almost completely defenseless the crab's soft-shell makes it easier for foragers to crush. Throughout the summer soft-shell crabs spawn and the odor emitted by the crab's bright orange eggs becomes irresistible to their hungry neighbors.

Catching Crabs

The best way to catch crabs is with a galvanized crab net. These nets can be purchased at your local tackle store. Make sure all parts are well galvanized and rinse thoroughly with fresh water after each use. These nets trap crabs against the galvanized netting as a wave recedes. Look for white or light gray crabs. Touch each suspect crab to see if it is soft and pliable. Some may be as soft as warm butter. Others will be more like bending a pop can. Because they tend to slide, the softer the crab the harder it is to keep on the hook. Crabs that are too hard will not be eaten. I've found that medium-soft is the best bait.

Keep and transport your crabs in a waist bait bucket. A small piece of wet kelp helps to keep the temperature down and the bait fresh. If you plan to keep the crabs overnight cover them with some damp newspaper or kelp. Be sure not to crush them. I place the bucket in a cool dry place (the garage) and my wife appreciates that. By all means don't place them in salt water or refrigerate. Be sure to disturb them as little as possible or they will be cranky (and dead!) in the morning.

The best time to catch crabs is on a large incoming tide. Peak high tide is your most productive time. Time of day is not usually important unless there is excessive beach traffic that drives crabs down. When you first walk on the beach near the water, feel the sand with your bare feet. As you walk you'll notice that sand is soft or firm in different areas. Crabs like soft sand that is easy to burrow into and rely upon it until their hard shell develops.

In most cases, crabs live in the soft sand just below the high tide mark. As the water passes over them they climb to the surface to feed. Softer crabs break loose and can be caught. Being soft, they find it much harder to dig back in as the water recedes and are thus more vulnerable to predators and your crab net.

Where To Find Crabs

Sand crabs like soft sand. They don't like rock or pebbly areas. When you first reach the beach look down between the high tide mark and the ocean. Look for moving water areas. As the wave recedes look for little "Vs" in the sand. This is a field of crabs. Because crabs feed with their tails they are easy to see grouped in bunches and exposed as the water recedes between waves. The warmer the water, the closer they will be to the surface.

Look for patches of "tails." Approach the patch and wait for the water to rush over the area before standing on it. Once covered by water, step forward and place the net in the water and allow it to settle to the bottom. A surprise approach means crabs will be less likely to dig deeper into the sand and easier to catch. Continue as you crab to look up and down the beach to find more "tail" clusters.

The most effective method of using the crab net involves digging sand into the net with one foot, as the water recedes. This breaks the crabs loose from the sand and yields larger catches. Incoming and out going waves can both be used for catching crabs. Always remember that water must be running *out* of the net at all times or your bait will swim, crawl and disappear back into the sea.

Over the years I've seen all kinds of contraptions to catch crabs. One guy even told me that a net was cheating because it made crabbing too easy. No matter what you use, even your hands, crabs are the best surf bait around. Your local tackle shop will carry galvanized crab nets for around $50.00

Tip: *Catch* **hard-shell** *sand crabs in the summer and freeze them for use during the winter. Save the larger crabs. When defrosted they will be just about as soft as a shell-less crab. Remember, don't freeze soft crabs or you'll have mush!*

Hooking Your Bait
Each type of bait has its own special way to be hooked. No matter what bait you are using the most important word to remember is "presentation." Most of all you want to make the fish believe that the bait is occurring naturally. It doesn't matter how good your bait is – if it's floating upside down it won't get a bite.

It's always good to practice before or after a trip on hooking baits properly. Don't wait until you are in the middle of a great bite to try to figure out how to hook your bait.

Sand crabs can be hooked two ways. From front to back or from back to front. They can also have the hook protrude from the top of their shell or from the bottom of their shell.

Three steps to hooking crabs (enlarged hook used for display)

Choose a sharp hook that best matches the size of the bait. I prefer to use offset octopus hooks with a snell eye. I've found that snell tying the hook creates the strongest knot, good hook set and some elasticity. Octopus hooks come in silver, black and red. Red seems to work well in the dead of summer when surf fish are looking for egg laden soft shell sand crabs.

Place the hook through one end of the crab; either through the top of the shell or from the bottom between the legs. Pull the tip and the barb through the crab. Rotate the hook and place it through the opposite end of the crab. Be sure the hook end is sharp and protrudes so it will penetrate the fish. Sometimes when a bite slows I'll flip the crab over and hook it with the opposite side up. This changes the "presentation" and may attract more fish. Replace your sand crab when it has been partially eaten or after several casts with no bites.

Tip: *During the winter months, when crabs are long gone, you still can use them for bait! In a small zip bag combine 4 tablespoons of hot sauce and a dozen frozen sand crabs. It about twenty minutes you'll be ready to fish.*

When only small crabs are available try two or three on the hook at once.

Sidewinder Rock Crabs

You see these guys scurrying across the rocks as you walk out to your favorite fishing jetty. The sidewinder crab has always been great surf bait in California. At times they may be a bigger challenge to catch than to fish. This rock crab is green and brown in color. It possesses two large (and somewhat painful!) claws. They live between rocks in nooks, crannies and crevices.

The best place to find sidewinders is just above the waterline on rock jetties and tide pool areas. Look for them between mussel clusters, in crevices or by flipping over small rocks. These crabs can be found at both low and high tide. Due to their keen sight, once they detect motion, they scurry off. When approaching, move slowly. Stop, look and see where they are positioned on the rock. Pick out a single crab (after some practice, a bunch of crabs) and as you approach watch carefully as to where that crab ends up. Now that you've located the crab the best way to catch it is to pin it to the rock with your fingers. Get a grip and pull them from the rock to your waist bait bucket. Pinching hurts, so the best way to avoid that is to hold the crab by the back of its body pinching it between your thumb and forefinger. Start with one finger on top of the crab's back and one finger on the crab's underside. Hold him by the back with his claws forward.

Sidewinder crabs are very hardy and last quite a long time in the captivity of your garage. In fact, and I hate to admit it, when I was a kid, and ziptop bags were just introduced, one night surf fishing I lost track of a bag of crabs. One week later when I was surfing at the same spot I found *the* bag of crabs. To my amazement the crabs were alive.

Sidewinders, If kept in a cool plastic container with wet paper or burlap over them, will live for a solid week. Just enough time to slow their pinch down so you can get *"them"* on the hook without them getting you!

Catching the crab is hard. Thankfully, hooking the crab is much easier. As with most baits match your hook size with the size of the bait. On smaller crabs, I tend to use a short shank hook, like an octopus style, so the shank does not pull the bait sideways and effect the presentation. If the crab is larger I will use a worm hook. The worm hook's longer shank makes it easier to penetrate and hook the larger sidewinder crab.

Once again grasp the crab between your thumb and forefinger. Insert the sharp end of the hook into one of the leg sockets, through to the other side, or directly through the rear of the crab shell. This technique will insure the best presentation while keeping the crab firmly on the hook. Remember that it is always important to use sharp hooks and make sure the business end of the hook is protruding through the shell exposed to the barb.

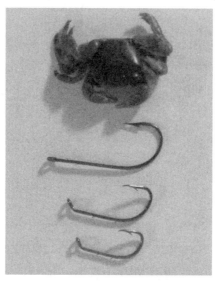

Match a worm or octopus hook to the size of your bait

Turn the crab over and insert hook through last leg socket

Pull hook through carefully and exit through the opposite leg socket

Rock And Piling Mussels

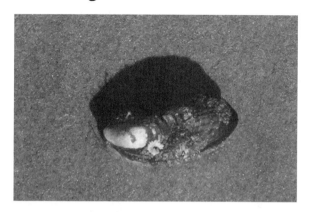

Mussels are found anywhere you have substantial tidal movement, in conjunction with rock, pilings or jetty structure. More than anywhere else, muscles seem to thrive on pier and platform pilings. But some of the biggest muscles, and probably the oldest, can be found on our local rock jetties.

The best time to collect mussels is at low tide. Take only as many as you'll need. You may collect extras, shuck the shells and freeze them for later use. I divide them into small zip top bags. This way I can use them without wasting what I've collected. Only thaw once. Mussels thawed and refrozen may become too mushy for bait.

When shucking mussel use a small knife to cut the tendons near the rear of the shell. On one side, near the back, there is a small indentation or hole. Insert your knife into this hole and slowly pull the knife forward toward the front of the shell. As you move along it will cut the tendon and once the shell is partly open you can pry it apart with your fingers.

Pier Mussel

Inside you will find two different bait textures. One very soft and pliable another very rubbery and strong. Both make good bait. When hooking mussel, I'll wrap it around an octopus hook (seems ironic!) and lastly pierce the rubber lip membrane until it holds the bait below the barb. This way the bait is firmly held in place and will stay on for a long hard cast.

Not unlike sidewinder crabs, mussel is very hardy and will last in a cool moist plastic tray for several days. They can be cleaned immediately or are a bit easier to shuck after being stored a few days. By all means, do not eat mussel. It's a filter organism that when feeding passes huge quantities of water through its membrane. It's "muscle" then retains and concentrates toxins it filters from the water.

For hooking mussel, use the same technique seen below for blood and lugworms. "Feed" mussel up the hook to make it appear like a worm. The lip membrane is the strongest and most elastic part of the mussel so use it to twist over the softer meat when placing on the hook. Be sure to puncture the lip membrane past the barb to hold it securely. Some anglers also use dental floss to secure mussel to the hook.

Baits You Catch With Cash

Bloodworms
Ghost Shrimp
Razor Clams
Lug Worms

Bloodworms, Ghost Shrimp, lugworms and razor clams are easy to find when they are carried in your local tackle store. Bloodworms, ghost shrimp and lugworms are alive and relatively fragile. Razor clams are usually fresh frozen and must be kept cool until used. The best way to keep worms and shrimp is to refrigerate them. These baits come in containers from the store. Handle and disturb them as little as possible. Worms and shrimp kept in your refrigerator will last two to five days. Worms are only effective bait when alive. Once dead, discard them. Worms do not freeze and when dead emit an order that repels fish.

Clams

Clams and mussels are hooked the same. Simply cut or pinch off a dime size piece and place on a short shank octopus style hook. This bait is very stable on the hook and is easy to cast. Change your bait periodically, more often if you are not getting bit. You'll find that clams are durable and attractive for perch and yellowfin croaker.

Ghost Shrimp

Ghost shrimp are fragile and can be tricky to hook. Shrimp are best kept in the refrigerator when not being used. Use a long shank worm hook for shrimp. Insert the hook near the shrimp's tail and "feed" the hook up through its body. Exit the business end of the hook to just above the barb just below the shrimp's head. Once again, change your bait periodically, more often if you are not having success. Ghost shrimp work great for perch, yellowfin croaker and corbina (In fact, it was the bait used for the current corbina world record).

Insert hook under tail

Feed hook up body

Exit hook and cast carefully

Blood and Lug Worms

Bloodworms differ from lugworms in several ways. Bloodworms are generally larger and have a stronger casing. They stay intact longer on the hook and can be used to catch several fish without changing the bait. Another worm choice is Lugworms, which are much less expensive, but tend to disintegrate after one or two fish. Both work great for perch, yellowfin croaker and corbina.

The technique used to hook worms is definitely an art. When it comes to hooking blood or lug worms it takes practice to get the bait hooked just right. The first step is to expel the creature from its tube lining. Inside the worm you'll find a set of four pinchers (two on lugworms). They appear as if they are tiny fingernails. The worm uses these to catch its prey and to dig holes in the sand. On larger worms these claws can get your attention as they clamp onto your skin with a sharp pinch.

It's essential to have the worm expose itself outside of the casing to hook it correctly. To avoid getting pinched I take my hemostats (i.e. stainless pliers) and pinch the worm's end to expose the pincers *or* rub the business end of the worm against my jacket to bring out the monster. The fresher the worm the faster and more pronounced the pincers and mouth will be.

> **Tip:** *Once the fish have reduced your bait to a one inch piece try using a small 1 1/2" grub below the worm on the hook. This drives perch nuts!*

To get the worm in a position to place on the hook I pinch (softly) the "neck" (below the mouth/pinchers) between my thumb and forefinger. Holding the worm firmly, insert the sharp hook end into the mouth (in the center of the pinchers). Slowly and carefully, trying not to puncture the worm casing, feed the worm up the hook. Pull the worm onto the hook until you reach the hook eye and mono knot. Firmly grasp the mouth and pull it over the hook eye. At this point the worm can also be slipped up the line. Leaving a one and one-half inch end, puncture the hook through the worm casing. Be sure to pull the hook past the barb so it sets well and will hold the worm in place as you cast.

Hooking Worms

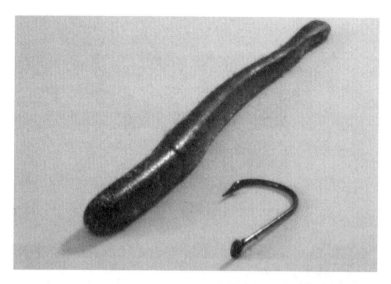

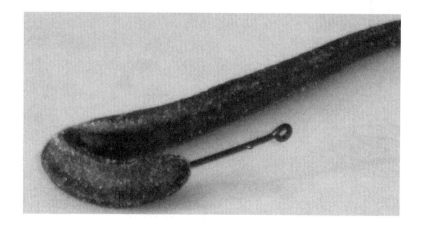

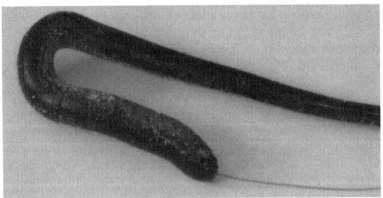
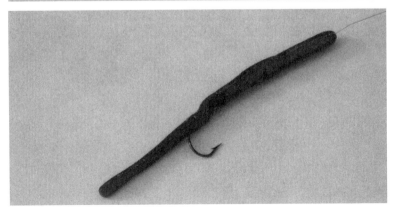

After a few bites, check your worm and see if you need to slide a new tail end down again. You can do this by retracting the hook from the worm casing, pulling the worm back off the hook, about one and one-half inch and then puncturing it back through the side casing. This again leaves a small tail dangling for presentation. Be sure to pull the business end of the hook through to the barb. With some practice you'll be able to catch more than one fish on each bait. Leaving the bait in one piece not only makes it easier to use but also gives the worm a more natural presentation and catches more fish.

Tip: *Soak a handful of lug worms in an inch of milk and within 24 hours they will double in size!*

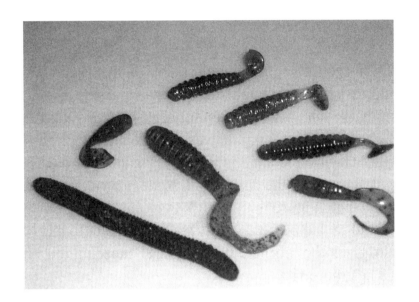

Artificial Baits
Grubs
Flies
Lures

Artificial baits come in many shapes, sizes, materials and colors. *Remember rule number one: always match your bait to what occurs naturally in the area you are fishing.* But also, don't be surprised if something that seems unnatural for the area works too. Look for lures that are similar in shape and color. Opt for darker lures if you're not sure of the exact color — darker trout-sized lures are useful because they cast an enticing shadow to fish in almost any light situation.

Although there are many artificial lures, the most commonly used in local waters include grubs, spoons and flies.

Grubs and flies can be used year round but seem to work best during winter months when the water is colder and bait is scarce. Spoons seem to work best during the summer months when the water is warmer and fish are chasing anchovies, sardines, smelt, grunion and fry in the surf.

Grubs are nothing more than a small plastic worm. Their color attracts fish and their tail entices them to bite. The most productive size of grub is two inches. Remember to match the grub size to local bait. If you fish with a larger size and get no bites go to a smaller grub. Grubs generally have three common tails: straight, curly and stumped.

Curly

Stump

Curly and stumped tails give the lure more action and are more productive in daylight hours. Straight tail is much like a short worm and seems to work best after dark.

Use different grub colors depending on the color of the water you are fishing. If you throw the wrong color you might as well be dragging a spark plug out there.

TIP: *The most productive grub colors are: Smoke with glitter, motor oil glitter, watermelon/chartreuse, pearl green/silver glitter, sour grape, caterpillar, avocado, green pumpkin, green/pearl and pumpkin with black flake*

With waves crashing and locally churned murkiness, most surf fishing areas have cloudy water. Whites and muted colors can not be seen and won't work. Dark colors, which cast a more enticing shadow, match surrounding bait and work best. Motor oil, red flake, gray flake and brown seem to do the job.

Hooking the grub is very similar to stringing a worm—with one big exception-NO pinchers! First, place the hook against the outside of the grub to get an idea of where the hook's end will punch through the grub body. Begin by pushing the sharp hook end into the very middle of the grub's head.

Check the grub to see if the grub has lines, like a seam, left by the mold. If so, be sure to center your penetration between these lines. Holding the grub between thumb and forefinger feed the hook down toward the tail and exit with the sharp end. Once most of the shaft is buried in the plastic grub, stop. Carefully, pull the grub head back toward the hook eye. This will even-out the grub and help to flatten it onto the hook. Again, think about presentation. The more the grub looks like it's flat and freely moving through the water (without a hook!) the better chance you'll get a bite. Check your grub every other cast (every cast if you get a bite) to be sure it's flat and tracking best through the water. Do this by pulling the grub back and forth in front of you to see how it tracks through the water. It's shaped to swim naturally and should look that way.

Hold the hook next to the grub to see where the hook will exit the bait

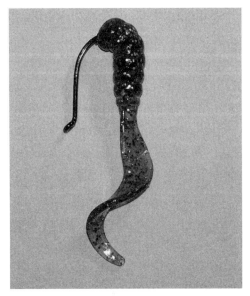

Begin threading the hook through the middle of the grub toward the tail

Finish by exiting and pulling the grub straight onto the hook

The best way to present the grub is by using the sliding rig. In larger surf a shorter leader is best because it helps to keep your bait near the bottom. As with all surf baits it is important to have contact with the bottom at all times.

Tip: (***Hot sauce tip #2***)*When fishing the grub (just like with an unfrozen sand crab) cover it with hot sauce from your local taco stand—you'll be amazed how well it works! Reapply after several casts.*

Flies

Flies are still somewhat of a mystery to me. By far my most effective fly has been the Clauser Minnow, a two-eyed minnow shaped fly about two inches long. My favorite colors are off white with motor oil green. As with all hooks, make sure your fly hook is sharp.

The best way to rig the fly on a spinning rod is to use the smallest sliding egg sinker (one-quarter to one-half ounce) and a twenty-four inch six pound test leader. The Clauser is effective for perch, halibut, stripped bass and corbina. Fish the fly in the same manner as with the grub. Slowly retrieving your rig along the bottom will help sink the weight into the sand. Unlike worm fishing, use a long leader to help keep your fly up off the bottom.

Lures

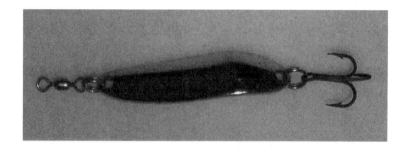

A wide variety of lures work well in the surf. One common denominator for all these lures is that they *must be trout-sized, shiny and flash* when retrieved through the water. In the murky bubbly surf zone, silver flashing helps attract fish to bait they can't smell.

Krocodile®, Kastmaster® and needlefish work well with a slow retrieval. In Mexico, crocodile lures are used as large as two ounces. But in our local surf the smaller one-half ounce model is the best size. Where as grubs are most productive in winter months, lures are most productive in the summer. Halibut often mistake the shiny lure for wounded bait in the days following a grunion run.

Keeping Bait Alive and Fresh

Sand crabs, sidewinders, and mussel
Keep in a shallow plastic container with a small piece of kelp adjacent to the bait (a moist towel also works). The container should be kept in a cool dry place (like your garage) and disturb as little as possible. Keep moist but *do not* immerse in salt water. Sand crabs will live for two to three days. Sidewinders and mussel will stay alive and fresh for up to seven days. Mussels can also be kept in a damp burlap sack.

I freeze a small bottle of water and place it into, but not against, the bait inside a small ice chest. A cool undisturbed place helps bait live longer.

Bloodworms, Lugworms, and Ghost Shrimp
Keep refrigerated. Do not freeze. Undisturbed bait will live for two to seven days in your refrigerator. When undisturbed, lugworms will live up to fourteen days— or about twice as long as bloodworms and ghost shrimp. Place bags or boxes of bait in a brown paper bag. When returning from fishing put bait in the refrigerator as soon as possible. When worms die put them in the trash. Once again, dead worms are no good because they excrete an odor when dead that does not attract fish.

Freezing Bait

Being prepared by freezing bait a day or week before a fishing trip can make the difference between catching fish or not.

Each package should contain enough for one day's fishing. I place mussel and pre-cut strips of squid together and freeze in a small snack-size zip top bag. Frozen squid and mussel become tougher after freezing and are easier than fresh to keep on the hook.

When the fishing day is over and you won't be going back to the beach tomorrow, toss your leftover worms in the trash. Worms cannot be frozen.

Sand crabs, sidewinders and ghost shrimp should all be frozen separately in small one-day size packages. Ghost shrimp tend to get mushy so freeze them as soon as you get back from fishing.

Place bait packages in labeled brown paper bags in the freezer. Don't be surprised if your wife or girl friend finds them and throws them out. To avoid this, it might be good to invest in your own freezer for the garage! ***Once per year throw out old bait and start over.***

Notes:

CHAPTER 4

Gear Up

In This Chapter:

Lines And Leaders
Sinkers
Swivels
Hooks
Beads
Knot tying
Rigging

This chapter is dedicated to the craft of the surf rig. A lot has changed from the days when we employed the dropper loop and a four-ounce pyramid sinker-cluster bomb! Today's surf fisherman uses lighter and more selective tackle to target the most exciting species of surf fish.

Terminal Tackle
Terminal tackle includes line, sinker, swivel, hook and bead.

Lines And Leaders
To prepare your rigging you'll need some terminal tackle. The first item to consider is your line and leader material. The monofilament on your spinning reel should be strong and flexible. I prefer Ande® line in pink, green or clear. Pink being my favorite because it fades as it wears and is easy to see when it needs replacing. Its color also resembles the churned water of the Southern California surf.

Lines like Ande®, Maxima® and Berkeley® all work well because they stretch and act like a shock absorber when the fish is brought across the inshore trough. Stiffer lines tend to kink easily and snap when pounded by waves. Four to twelve pound test line (*four to six* for sand and twelve for rocky shores). Pink, green and clear colors all work well in the surf. When fishing around rocky areas clear or green seem to work best.

When spooling your spinning reel up with monofiliment, always feed the new line off the end of the spool and onto your reel. By placing the new spool on its side the new line will have a slight twist and explode off the reel while casting. (*see diagram below*)

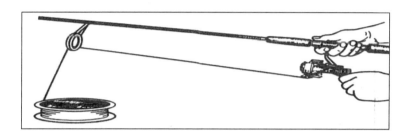

Several factors go into how long your line will last. Reels kept out of the sun and washed off with fresh water will always last longer. After each trip to the beach rinse your outfit off with a soft spray from the hose or a misting bottle and dry off immediately. This helps eliminate the salt and sand build up on your line, reel and rod.

I use a quart spray bottle filled with two tablespoons of dish soap and water to wash off my rod and reel. An old white cotton sock over your hand works well to dry off your rig. I also spray a small amount of lubricant (c.f. Corrosion X®) on a sock and wipe down the reel to leave it with a thin oil coating to protect and lubricate.

Sinkers

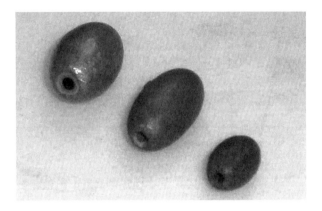

Egg sinkers and split shot sinkers are the most commonly used weights. Egg sinkers weighing one-quarter to three-quarters ounce are the most common size. Remember to use the heavier sinkers in strong drift, wind and surf conditions. Smaller sinkers are best for very calm days and give your bait the most life-like movement.

Egg sinkers work particularly well in the surf because their freedom of movement on the line. This helps when pulling the fish through the surf. Additionally, this small sinker will bury itself in the sand, especially during the retrieve, and make it harder for the fish to see.

A split shot can be used with sand crabs for Corbina. This method uses the ocean's surge to roll the bait in and out in very shallow water where the corbina feeds. Much like flylining a live bait.

Swivels

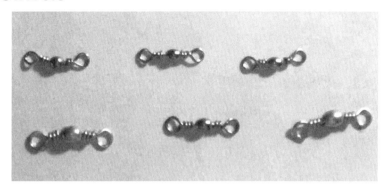

Swivels are used as the connection between your leader and the main line. It acts as a stop for the bead and sinker by keeping them well above the hook. Use the smallest swivel possible. Brass is fine in a size six to ten.

Hooks

There are two basic surf hooks I use:
Long shank worm and *snell-eyed octopus hooks.*

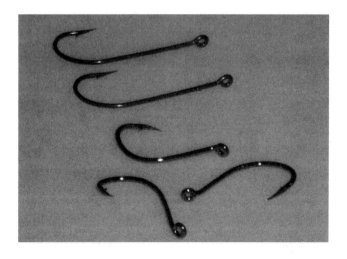

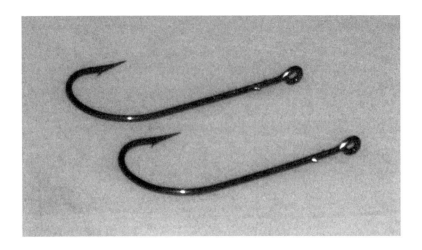

Long shank hooks are used for worm threading. The longer shaft makes its easier to pull the eye up and through the worm. I use a size one for larger bait and two for smaller worms. Long shank hooks also work well with larger plastic grubs, ghost shrimp, large sidewinder crabs and with mussel. Black/non zinc hooks rust faster in your tackle bag but disintegrate and fall out quicker when they need to be left in a fish.

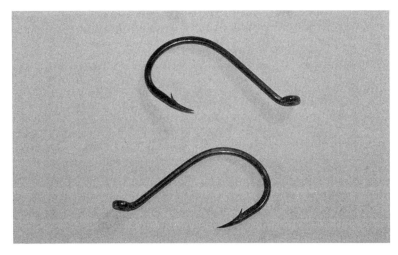

Octopus snell-eyed hooks are for sand crabs, grubs and small sidewinders. Match the hook size to the size of the bait. Small crabs will use a size six hook. Larger sand crabs could require a number one. I pre-tie several leader rigs for easy changing. They are kept on a leader holder that fits in your pocket.

I use a snell-eyed hook for crabs because it gives the bait a more realistic presentation and because a snelled knot snugs tighter the harder the fish fights.

Tip: *The wily corbina's keen sight requires that you use a hook small enough to be hidden from sight inside the bait*

Hooks are best kept in their original package. Do not return a hook to the pack if it has touched salt water. The salt will react and begin the rust process on all the hooks it touches. Hooks also need to be kept sharp. You can reuse hooks and leaders, but after a couple of visits to the beach, throw them out. Once engaged in salt water and sunshine hooks will immediately begin to break down.

Beads

Beads come in several sizes. A medium to large bead is used between the sliding sinker and the swivel. This is to cushion the sinker from the swivel and allow the sinker to move more freely. As a fish attractant, small beads can be used on the leader, just above the hook when fishing with sand crabs or grubs. Both should be red or orange beads. Orange preferred because they imitate the egg sacks on a sand crab's underside.

OTHER GEAR

Hemostats are also known as surgical clamps. Hemostats are used to remove hooks from fish. They make it easier to reach down into the fish's throat and safely remove the hook. They can also be used to help hold and expel a bloodworm's pinchers. To retard rust be sure the hemostats are stainless steel.

Line clippers (fingernail) are best kept on a lanyard. They are used to cut and trim main lines and leaders.

Waist bait keeper is a plastic bait holder with a belt to attach around your waist.

Measuring tape is used to measure the size of your fish.

Sand crab traps can be found at your local tackle shop. Make sure the trap is well built and galvanized. Always rinse with fresh water after each use.

Small zip top bags are used to carry various sizes of hooks, beads, swivels, grub tails and flies.

Disposable or digital camera is a must, because with catch and release, a camera is a quick way to record your record catch.

Neck wallet or fanny pack is what I carry my gear in at the beach. If I'm fishing a sandy beach the neck wallet can hold plenty of gear. If I'm fishing the rocks or an area that requires heavier gear I'll use the fanny pack. Keeping equipment light and comfortable makes it a lot easier as you stroll the beach stalking the big one.

Knots

Improved Clinch

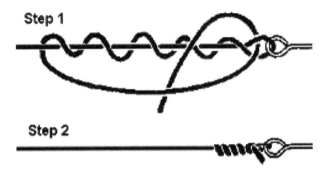

Snell Knott

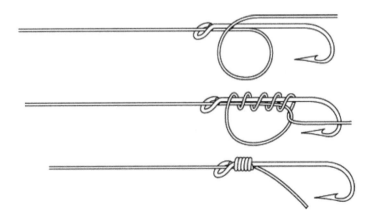

Spider Hitch

Surf Rigs

Carolina Rig

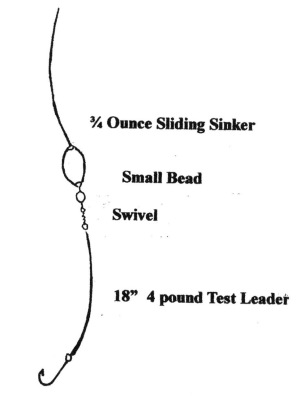

¾ Ounce Sliding Sinker

Small Bead

Swivel

18" 4 pound Test Leader

Octopus Or Worm Hook

Application: Live bait, grub, and fly. In larger surf use a shorter leader and more weight. Leader can be mono or straight fluorocarbon. Try a little variation; in the winter I will use a very small orange bead above my hook and *below* the swivel. It sits on the hook eye, just above the grub.

Halibut Stinger

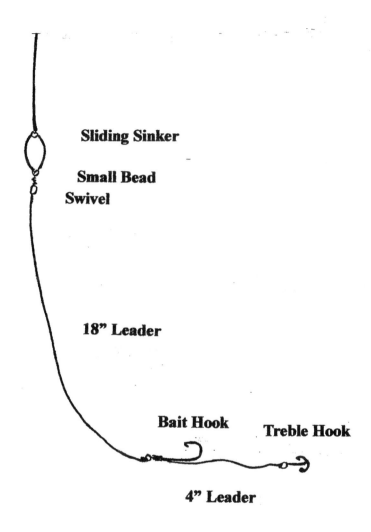

Application: Live or fresh-dead bait. Hook sardine or anchovy across the nose with the bait hook. Place the treble, barb deep, into one side of the bait's tail.

Split Dropper Loop

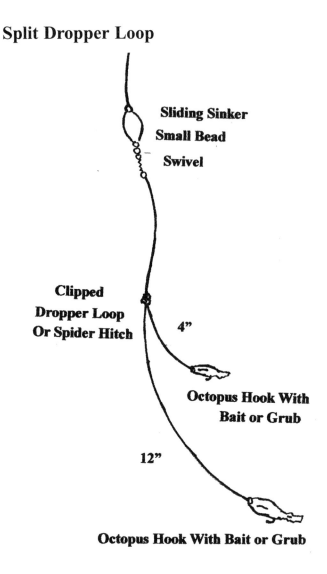

Application: Bait or Grub. Tie a dropper loop or spider hitch and clip it so one tag end will finish at 4" and the other at 12". Works with a slow retrieve as with the Carolina Rig.

CHAPTER 5

Taking Control

In This Chapter

**Fighting the fish
Fishing in the wind**

Fighting The Fish

Fighting a large fish on the beach, with surf and surging water, is like nothing you've ever done before.

Most fish hooked from the surf don't head straight out. Rather, they tend to swim parallel to the beach. As they move in an up or down-shore direction they can use the swell and surge to their advantage.

The best way to fight fish in these shore beak conditions is to first back up, once you're hooked up, and use the rise on the beach for leverage.

Rule number one would be to always keep your line taught with a bend in the rod. Pull the fish toward you using the incoming waves (as you do with a rising and falling boat). Slow or stop retrieving completely when the waves are flushing out. As the fish reaches the shallows (two feet of water or in the inshore trough) move forward toward the water always keeping your line taught and the rod bent.

As you move closer to the water always keep a wary eye on the size and timing of the shore break. Nothing is worse than losing sight of the next wave and becoming the next victim. *Know were you are in relationship to the waves.* Use the shore break to bring the fish closer to you and not you closer to the fish.

Once the fish is in the very shallows (about one foot of water) stop reeling and slowly walk back up the beach dragging the fish with you. If you have an exceptionally strong sucking out of water or a large fish you may have to retreat again toward the ocean and play the fish back and forth until it is tired enough to come up onto the sand.

With larger fish, the ying and yang of landing your catch is a real test of patience and finesse. Fighting fish from the beach is a challenge but with experience you'll develop a feel for it and know when the time is right to move toward and away from the foaming water. With practice you'll get good at landing your catch on the beach and be surprised by the size of fish the receding water leaves behind.

Wind (The Great Equalizer)

Fish really have an edge when it comes to the wind. Onshore or side shore wind makes it more difficult to feel bites and react to them.

With light test line you want to be tight with the bottom so you can feel bites and bottom structure. Lighter lines also tend to stretch more and make it more difficult to get a good hookset. To be successful with surf fishing you must always have you line tight to your sinker.

When it's windy a bow appears in your line and delays the strike feeling as the fish picks up your bait. In turn, it also delays your hookset movement from reaching the fish.

The best way to fish wind swept conditions is to keep your line taught by casting straight into the wind. After casting, keep your line low to the sand to reduce wind resistance. Do not fish up sand unless you're hooked up and want to us the leverage provided by the rise. Keep low to the wind. Remember, constant retrieval of your line is essential to keeping the line taught and feeling the bites. Always use more weight in these applications to make sure your bait remains in constant contact with the bottom.

It also helps to pull your line and bait in the direction the wind is blowing. Many times the drift (caused by waves and wind) is too strong for fish to catch up with your bait. In these cases, cast into the wind and walk slowly along the beach keeping your line in front of you as it drifts along.

Unlike onshore winds, winds blowing offshore are ideal and have little effect on fishing technique. In addition, they provide better visibility for the fisherman. Offshore winds help to "clean up" the ocean surface and make the water clearer. Some of my best surf fishing has been in fall and during California's famous Santa Ana winds.

CHAPTER 6

Tide and Moon

In This Chapter

**What Causes Tides
What Tide Is Best For Surf Fishing
How To Read Tide Charts
Tides And Time Of Day
The Moon's Affect On Surf Fishing**

Tidal movement and moon phase are one of the least understood natural phenomenon yet they have one of the most pronounced influences on surf fishing. Higher tides expose more food and provide more underwater structure than low tides. Full moon phases give fish more light to feed and can dramatically change the hours of day found to be the most productive.

What Causes Tides

It is important to understand tidal and moon phases because of their pronounced affect on the quality of fishing. Tidal theory includes the interaction between gravitational and centrifugal forces. The earth's inwards pull, know as gravity, is balanced by the earth, moon and sun's daily rotation. Although, in the greater sense these are in equilibrium (or else we would spin off into the universe!). They are not quite in balance because of the Earth's uneven surface, and as a result, create tidal movement.

As the Earth moves in elliptical rotation the sun's gravitational pull is greater in areas that are closer to the sun. These areas experience high tides as the Earth's water stretches to meet the strong gravitational pull. When areas on the Earth are farther from the sun this causes low tides as the sun's influence on the oceans is lessened. Additionally, because the earth rotates on its axis at a slight tilt, the highs and lows will not normally occur at the same levels each day. Likewise the gravitational pull of the moon also affects tidal movement. The movement and rotation of both the sun and moon work simultaneously to raise and lower bodies of water on Earth.

Another phenomenon that affects fishing is the astronomical tide. At the new and full moon the combined gravitational pull of the sun and moon causes the greatest tidal variation. These are called Spring or Astronomical Tides. These tides generally occur on a BI-yearly basis when the sun and moon are there closest to Earth. This phenomenon enhances the tidal variation leading to the largest yearly tidal swings. Besides the normal flooding and nuisance they cause they also have a dramatic effect on fishing.

In the following sections we will learn which tides are best for surf fishing and how to read tide charts.

What Tide Is Best For Surf Fishing

The optimal tide would allow for roughly a six-foot tidal swing. For example, a morning high tide of 6.2 feet and an afternoon low tide of 0.2 feet would allow for this six-foot swing. Tidal movements greater than this leads to strong upcoming and receding water movement. Movement which makes it difficult for fish to see and catch bait. Tidal movement less than this, and especially during diurnal or neap (small swing) tides, cause the opposite condition—very little water movement and thus much less rotation of bait through the strike zone.

With rare occasion, the best time to surf fish is on an upcoming high tide. Two hours before through two hours after the high tide. Although fish can be caught during the low tide cycle, there tends to be less bait movement and living structure available at these times.

During the slack high tide period (the time exactly when the high tide is reached) water movement is also at a minimum and many times the bite will fade away and then become dramatically active again as water begins to move, receding on the low tide cycle.

Tip: *The largest tidal changes are during the full and new moon phase. This will cause the largest movement of water and provide both opportunity and challenge to the fisherman. Some of the best fishing and bait catching conditions occur during these moon phases.*

How To Read Tide Charts

Tide charts can be found at your local tackle store, surf shop or on the Internet. They come in small pocket sized books or in the form of a graphic calendar. I prefer tides presented in graph form as seen in the following illustrations. This format makes it very easy to visualize the changes in tidal movement and thus plan your trip accordingly.

Below are graphic calendar illustrations of tidal movement. One of the first things you'll notice using a graph is that the best fishing tides occur roughly every two weeks.

Semi-diurnal tides (The Best Fishing Tide)

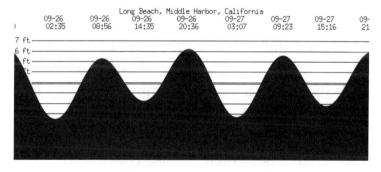

Large water movement

Diurnal (neap) tides (The Least Desirable Tide)

Very little water movement

Tides And Time Of Day

Unlike other species we fish for (especially the White Sea bass) the time of day for surf fishing is not as important. If I had a preference I would always want to fish at sunrise and sunset. But many surf fish, and especially the corbina, have very little interest in the time of day. Some of my best catches have been in mid morning to early afternoon. But with that said, the time of day is important when combined with the "people factor".

There is no doubt that the "people factor" comes in to play when fishing the beach. In the summer time, when the beach is most crowded, loads of little feet pound the sand and the stomping and splashing frightens fish. At these times I do fish early and late when the water is calm and the fish come close inshore to feed. At times when I must fish during "people factor" conditions I fish only the areas that are least crowded. This helps to avoid the finicky fish and the parent who assumes I'll hook their kid.

TIP: The best time to surf fish is when the tidal movement has at least a six foot swing, on an upcoming high tide, two hours before until two hours after peak high tide and in the evening or morning when the "people factor" is not a factor.

The Moon's Affect On Surf Fishing

Very little is known about how the moon affects fishing. Many long-range fisherman swear by the notion that a full moon means a great bluefin tuna bite. But this is mostly a myth with very little scientific backing.

One thing we do know about the moon phase is during a full moon fish feed at night because they are able to see and track bait. During new moon periods (when the moon is dark) fish feed in the very early morning and evening when the light is bright enough to see their food but low enough to hide them as predator.

In general, full moon nights mean surf fishing will be better later in the day, and particularly in the afternoon. The biological clock for fish is pushed back while they digest what they have found and caught during the previous moonlight filled night.

Notes:

CHAPTER 7

Catch and Release

In This Chapter

How To Safely Release Fish

Do you catch and release?
Anglers catching fish to be released are urged to use methods that minimize the damage to the fish. Here are a few tested tips that will help you with the release process:

1. Wet hands before touching the fish

2. If possible, avoid grabbing and handling the fish body

3. Don't cover your fish with a towel

4. Avoid letting the fish hit the boat deck or rail

5. Whenever possible, keep your fish in the water when releasing the hook

6. When releasing the fish place it in the water gently. If the fish does not swim away move it slowly back and forward to force water into and through its gills

7. Consider pinching off barbs when the bite is hot and fish will be released

8. Cut your line when the fish is deeply hooked, your hook will rust out in a short time

9. Use circle hooks and single hook jigs, which cause much less damage and hook fish securely in the corner of the mouth

10. Keep fish to eat that are deeply hooked and bleeding profusely

11. Only keep what you want to eat and a small amount to freeze.

By releasing our fish back into the ocean we will help to upgrade our current fish stock and provide for better fishing for everyone in the future. Please practice catch and release fishing!

SURF FISH CALENDAR

FISH	JANUARY	FEBRUARY	MARCH	APRIL	MAY	JUNE	JULY	AUGUST	SEPTEMBER	OCTOBER	NOVEMBER	DECEMBER
CORBINA	☺	☺	☺	☺	☺☺	☺☺	☺☺☺	☺☺☺	☺☺	☺	☺	☺
YELLOW FIN CROAKER	☺	☺	☺	☺	☺☺	☺☺☺	☺☺☺	☺☺☺	☺☺☺	☺☺☺	☺☺	☺
BAR SURF PERCH	☺☺☺	☺☺☺	☺☺☺	☺☺	☺☺	☺☺	☺☺	☺☺	☺☺	☺☺☺	☺☺☺	☺☺☺
WALLEYE SURF PERCH	☺☺☺	☺☺☺	☺☺☺	☺☺	☺☺	☺☺	☺☺	☺☺	☺☺	☺☺☺	☺☺☺	☺☺
HALIBUT	☺	☺	☺☺	☺☺	☺☺☺	☺☺☺	☺☺	☺☺	☺☺	☺☺☺	☺	☺

☺ **Nothing to write home about but anything is possible**
☺☺ **Good solid fishing**
☺☺☺ **Call the boss and tell him you'll be late for work-it's fishin' time**

Notes:

Notes:

Notes:

Notes:

Notes: